ENGLISH LECTURE SERIES 英語説法シリーズ

Ryuho Okawa

Power to the Future

――― 未来に力を ―――

大川隆法

Preface

Now is the time for "Justice."

And the time for "Decision."

We need "Aspiration" to create our future.

The Power of God shall appear in the near future.

"Future" itself will have the power.

I myself shall realize the concept of God by my words.

I hope you all be able to receive "Positive Future" through this book.

Yes, you can!

March 20, 2013

World Teacher　Ryuho Okawa

（和訳）序文

　今こそ「正義」の時である。
　そして「決断」の時でもある。
　私たちが未来を創り出すには、「志」が必要である。
　神の力がもうすぐ姿を現すだろう。
　「未来」そのものが力を持つ時がくるのだ。
　私は、言葉を通じて神の概念を地に打ち立てるだろう。
　わが願いは、「積極的未来」を、あなたがたに与えることだ。この本を読むことを通して。
　そう、きっとできるだろう！

2013 年 3 月 20 日

世界教師(せかいきょうし)　大川隆法(おおかわりゅうほう)

Contents

(目次)

	Preface	1
	(和訳) 序文	2

Chapter One: Be Strong

1	Words Have Power	16
2	Japan is Facing an Imminent Danger of Invasion	17
	Happy Science has made great progress	17
	Warnings about the future: *The Final Judgement* and *The Mystical Laws*	18
	We must protect the beautiful country of Japan	21
3	We Must Have Criteria for Justice	22
	"We are sorry" is inexcusable	22
	What kind of a country is blessed by God?	24

	We need a new "Independence Day"	25
	A country cannot live on pacifism alone	27
	The world requires a new philosophy on peace and justice	28
4	**Be Strong and Take Responsibility**	29
	With great power comes great responsibility	29
	People who can take responsibility are strong people	31
	Responsibility comes from self-confidence, daily efforts and strong aspiration	31

(和訳) 第1章　強くあれ

1	言葉には力がある	34
2	侵略の危機が近づいている日本	35
	大発展してきた「幸福の科学」	35
	「近未来の恐怖」を警告した二つの映画	36
	日本は守るべき「美しい国」	39

3　「正義」についての基準を持て　　40

「遺憾です」という言い訳は許されない　　40

「神から祝福されている国」の見分け方　　42

日本人には「新しい独立記念日」が必要　　43

「平和主義」だけでは国が滅びる　　44

新しい「平和と正義の哲学」が
求められている　　46

4　責任を取れる「強い人」となれ　　47

「大きな力」には「大きな責任」が伴う　　47

強い人とは「責任を取れる人」のこと　　48

「自信」「日々の努力」「強い志」が必要　　49

Chapter Two: Love and Justice

1　Justice: An Urgent Matter for the Japanese
54

2 Japan's Confidence Shaken by the Takeshima and Senkaku Islands Issues 55

Xi Jinping aims to expand his "empire" 55

South Korea controls Takeshima as a symbol of its independence 56

The reason behind China's allegation of its authority over Senkaku Islands 58

China became more aggressive in response to Japan's nationalization of Senkaku Islands 60

Takeshima and Senkaku Islands: a struggle of the balance of power in Asia 62

3 The Happiness Realization Party Has Been Claiming the Need for National Defense 64

4 The Danger of Losing Senkaku Islands 66

China will surely set up missile facilities on Senkaku Islands 66

Japan's SLOC under threat means no crude oil for Japan 68

5	**Why Japan Must Preserve Nuclear Power Plants**	70
	Real cause of the Fukushima NPP accident: breakdown of emergency cooling generators	70
	In order to solve the energy problem, we should not act based on emotions	73
6	**Japan Must Debate More Strongly Against Foreign Countries**	75
	China and North Korea's possession of nuclear missiles allows them to threaten Japan	75
	"200,000 comfort women" is impossible	76
	The Koreans and the Chinese like to debate, but the Japanese do not	78
7	**Establish Justice by the Power of Wisdom**	79
	To stop evil deeds is an act of good and an act of justice	79
	Think of love from the viewpoint of wisdom	80

(和訳) 第2章　愛と正義

1　日本人にとって
　緊急を要する「正義」の問題　　　　　　　　83

2　「竹島・尖閣問題」で揺れる日本　　　　　　84
　"帝国"の拡大を目論む習近平　　　　　　　　84
　「独立の象徴」として
　竹島を実効支配する韓国　　　　　　　　　　85
　中国が「尖閣の領有権」を
　主張し始めた理由　　　　　　　　　　　　　87
　尖閣国有化を機に
　激しくなった「中国の反応」　　　　　　　　89
　「竹島・尖閣」は
　アジアのパワーバランスの問題　　　　　　　91

3　「国防」を訴え続けている幸福実現党　　　　92

4　尖閣を失うことの危険性　　　　　　　　　　93
　中国は尖閣に
　「ミサイル施設」をつくるはず　　　　　　　93

シーレーンが脅かされ、
石油が入らなくなる　　　　　　　　　　95

5　日本が「原発」を維持すべき理由　　　97
事故の本当の原因は「冷却用電源の喪失」　97

エネルギー問題は
「感情論」で動くべきではない　　　　　100

6　もっと強い姿勢で外国と討論を　　　101
「核」を背景に日本を脅してくる
中国と北朝鮮　　　　　　　　　　　　101

「20万人の従軍慰安婦」などありえない　102

日本人と違って討論を好む
韓国人や中国人　　　　　　　　　　　104

7　「智慧の力」によって正義を確立せよ　　105
悪行を止めることは「善」であり、「正義」　105

「智慧の視点」から愛を考えよう　　　　106

Chapter Three: Power to the Future

1   **Three Hypotheses Regarding the Future of the World**   110

2   **Western Countries Take Economically Shrinking Policies**   112

    Japan still has potential for the future   112

    Japan in the 1990s: a learning material for the EU   113

    Obama does not have a sufficient economic policy   115

3   **China is on the Verge of an Economic Debacle**   117

    China does not have enough financial knowledge and experience   117

    What Japan needs in order to defend against Chinese invasion   118

    China will dissolve starting from Hong Kong   120

4	South Korea Needs to Consider Itself as "A Member of the West"	122
5	We Must Gain the Strength to Conquer Evil	124
	China does not understand the meaning of liberty	124
	Fight against bad systems which are not loved by God	126

(和訳) 第3章　未来に力を

1	世界の未来に関する「三つの仮説」	128
2	経済において縮小政策をとる欧米	130
	日本には、まだまだ「未来の可能性」がある	130
	「1990年代の日本」に学ぶべき欧州連合	131
	十分な経済政策を持っていないオバマ氏	133
3	経済崩壊の危機に瀕する中国	135

中国には、金融についての
「知識と経験」が足りない　　　　　　　135

日本が「中国の侵略」を防ぐために
必要なこと　　　　　　　　　　　　　136

中国の解体は「香港(ホンコン)」から始まる　　　138

4　韓国は「西側の一員」としての自覚を　　140

5　悪を打ち負かす「強さ」を身につけよ　　141

「自由」の意味が分かっていない中国　　141

神に愛されていない「悪(あ)しき体制」と戦え　143

Chapter One

Be Strong
（強くあれ）

Lecture Given in English on June 12, 2012
at Happy Science General Headquarters
Happy Science, Tokyo

（2012年6月12日　東京都・幸福の科学総合本部にて）

1 Words Have Power

Today, I want to talk about "Be Strong."

I first started giving lectures overseas in November 2007, in Hawaii, with "Be Positive." Now I want to talk to you regarding "Be Strong." In this modern world, this is a very important topic for you to know about.

You are busy, of course, in your studies and in your business, but be strong and hold these two words in your mind every day. I think this is very important. It is a very short sentence, but it will make you brave and lead you to be a courageous man or woman.

These are just words, but words have power. They sometimes lead you to depression and

Be Strong

sometimes to a good condition. The outcome depends on the words that occur in your mind. This means that words are very important. I believe so.

2 Japan is Facing an Imminent Danger of Invasion

Happy Science has made great progress
I have experienced many things in these twenty-six years since I set up Happy Science.*

Now, we have more than 500 local temples, branches and missionary centers in Japan. In order to be active in our religious movement, we have many places for our activities in almost 100 countries. We also have many Shoshinkans

---
* Dates and titles are at the time of the lecture.

(main temples of Happy Science). There are more than twenty-five Shoshinkans in Japan.

In addition, we started the Happy Science Academy more than two years ago, and now we are scheduled to set up our next Happy Science Academy, a middle and high school, in Kansai (Opens April 2013).

Coming in 2015, we are also planning to set up the university version of the Happy Science Academy: the Happy Science University, in Chiba Prefecture.

Warnings about the future:
The Final Judgement **and** *The Mystical Laws*
Right now, at this moment, this June, we can see our latest movie, *The Final Judgement*, in

Be Strong

more than 200 places across Japan.

In this live-action movie, the main actor and actress portray the story of a religious resistance movement in Japan which is set in the near future.

It is one kind of a prediction movie and a science fiction film of sorts, but in reality it's not a far-fetched or imaginary story from the standpoint of pragmatic international politics. This movie depicts something which is a probability or a possibility in the near future.

We have another movie coming out this fall: *The Mystical Laws*. So, we have two movies this year (2012). Both of them are appealing to the Japanese people and, of course, the people from foreign countries surrounding Japan as well that a great and enormous omen can be seen in the near future. There will be an intruding power, an expanding power, and Japan is without doubt in imminent danger. This is what I think. We are announcing about the difficulties and fear in the near future. We must prepare for this.

The statesmen of Japan must state these things. Someone, obviously the head or the statesmen who are standing in higher positions, should speak out on such a kind of menace. By 'menace' I mean the countries which give rise to fear in Japan.

In Japan, however, there are just a few statesmen who can talk about such kinds of fear. Although we are a religious power and I am a religious person, I dare say that a crisis is coming soon and we must prepare for it.

We must protect the beautiful country of Japan

Japan now has a great power in itself, at least in terms of economic power. However, Japan does not have enough power in international politics, meaning in foreign diplomacy, due to a lack of confidence in recent Japanese history.

Japanese statesmen sometimes express their apologies toward other countries in Asia regarding World War II. But they do not awaken people about the coming crisis in Japan. Even if Japan did bad things several decades before, if another country were to do something similar towards Japan now, we, Japanese people, must prepare for the self-defense of our country because I love Japan.

Japan is a beautiful country and it has a long, traditional, cultural history. It is a heritage of the world. It must not be wiped out from this world, so we must defend against evil powers of other countries. This includes defending other small Asian countries as well. I believe so.

3 We Must Have Criteria for Justice

"We are sorry" is inexcusable

I dare say to you that history is history. Those who wrote the history books most definitely have right and wrong in them. However, the world history has been written entirely by the

Be Strong

people who achieved victory.

Therefore whether the description of history is correct or not isn't decided from the standpoint of, or in terms of, justice, but rather in terms of victory. That is the truth in history. So, history is history.

Now, in this age, we must have criteria for justice. Japanese people must be strong enough to have criteria for good and bad, and God and Evil. This is what I think.

No excuses can be allowed. Japanese statesmen sometimes give very good excuses. It is described in our film, *The Final Judgement*; they usually say, "We are very sorry about that." However, these are merely words. They say, "We are sorry about that, about the condition, about the occurrence of the worldwide event." It means almost nothing.

We must have some kind of standpoint, some kind of viewpoint which separates good from bad.

What kind of a country is blessed by God?
If there is a country where its people are living happily, freely and affluently, then such a country is good in itself and it should be guided by divine power. I believe so.

If the freedom of this kind of country is toasted by divine beings, then such a country should live on into the future. This is my thinking.

In the case of a bad country, if the government or the authority in that country suppresses its

Be Strong

people and does not allow people to protest or have the freedom of speech, freedom of press, freedom of religion or freedom of consciousness, then such kind of a country is not toasted by divine spirits. In other words, it is not blessed by God or Buddha.

We should make up our mind: "Which is good and which is bad?" "Which is true and which is false?" "Which is loved by God and which is disliked by God?"

We need a new "Independence Day"

We, Japanese people, must declare that Japan is an independent country. We need a new "Independence Day."

Japanese people experienced defeat in World

Power to the Future

War II more than sixty-seven years ago. We achieved independence after that, but have been relying too much on the United States of America. We just give them all the power to decide and tell what is good from bad. Almost all of this power is given away to the United States of America.

Yet, America is America. The United States is the United States. Japan is Japan. We, Japan, must decide by ourselves and for ourselves a policy concerning self-defense. That is why we have now dispatched our peaceful "weapon" in respect to our opinion about this recent crisis. This is the main content of *The Final Judgement*.

A country cannot live on pacifism alone

As a religious leader, I want to say that in the history of Buddhism, almost all Buddhists were peaceful and were pacifists. Almost all of them were pacifists in the political sense as well.

Despite that, for example, in old Burma or present-day Myanmar, there is a conflict between Islamic and Buddhist powers. Even Buddhists have the power of self-defense. They are accompanied by an army. If they didn't have that power, they would be easily destroyed by Islamic power because they would have no power to realize justice in this world.

In the old days, more than 2,500 years ago, I was born in Nepal and ran activities in India. In those times, as Buddha, I always taught you about pacifism and peace of mind.

I didn't like the intrusion of enemies or the destruction of the country. For example, my birthplace, the Shakya country, was destroyed by the neighboring, powerful country. It's very sad, but the people in the Shakya country were devotees of Buddhism. So, at that time, they were led to ruin without any resistance.

This tradition has continued for more than 2,000 years in the underlying trends of Buddhism.

The world requires a new philosophy on peace and justice

But yet, I dare say that there needs to be justice from the standpoint of world peace in Buddhism.

In reality, this should be the definition of justice of the U.N. If the U.N. works, its justice should bring peace all over the world, but it is not working properly at this time. The world requires a new philosophy regarding peace and justice.

I dare say that it depends on Happy Science. I will tell good from bad. I have this kind of might.

4 Be Strong and Take Responsibility

With great power comes great responsibility
I also recognize, "With great power comes great responsibility."

In other words, if you have a great power, it usually or inevitably is accompanied by great responsibility.

Japan and the Japanese people have great power in the world now, and this great power comes with great responsibility. This word 'come' means 'produce' or 'be accompanied by.'

For that reason, I want to say to the Japanese statesmen and statesmen-to-be, "You have a great power in the world now. This country has a great power. This country can save the economic crisis of the EU. If you can keep a good relationship with the United States, you can make a peaceful, pacifist world in the near future."

We have a great power. It means that this great power must be accompanied by great responsibility.

People who can take responsibility are strong people

In Japan, responsibility is essential. To have responsibility means you are not weak. You are not a weak person. You are not weak people.

People who can take responsibility are strong people. In terms of an individual, if you can take responsibility, it means that you are a strong man or a strong woman.

If you want to be strong, take responsibility.

Responsibility comes from self-confidence, daily efforts and strong aspiration

How can you take responsibility? This is the next problem. I'm sure you have this question.

Your responsibility shall be formed by your

self-confidence, daily efforts and strong aspiration.

I, myself, Ryuho Okawa, appear to be a normal person, but I am strong in my aspiration. This is the difference. I have a strong aspiration and strong willpower to make the world happier and more peaceful. We need willpower for that.

From now on, you must all think about the following: "With great power comes great responsibility. Great responsibility comes from your aspiration."

Nowadays in Japan, people sometimes talk about a "broken heart," not in the meaning of lost-love but in the meaning of abandoning aspiration. However, this is not good.

Be persistent and constructive in making a great custom every day. Make decisions based

Be Strong

on your will. Doing these things will lead you to your new power. This decision, or to take responsibility regarding your own course is a new power and I believe that this is the power to the future.

Power to the Future

(和訳) 第1章　強くあれ

1　言葉には力がある

　今日は、「強くあれ」ということについて述べたいと思います。

　私の海外での説法(せっぽう)は、2007年11月のハワイでの「Be Positive（積極的であれ）」から始まりましたが、今日は、「強くあれ」ということに関して、みなさんに話をしたいと思います。これは、みなさんにとって、ここ最近、非常に大事なことです。

　みなさんは、もちろん、勉強や仕事で忙(いそが)しいと思いますが、日々、強くあってください。この言葉を、日々、心のなかで思うことが非常に大事です。私は、そう思います。たいへん短い言葉ですが、この言葉は、みなさんを勇ましくし、勇気あ

る男性あるいは女性へと導くのです。

　これは単なる言葉にすぎません。しかし、言葉には「力」があるのです。言葉は、あるときは、みなさんを意気消沈させ、また、あるときは、みなさんを調子のよい状態へと導きます。それは、みなさんの心に浮かぶ言葉にかかっているのです。

　ですから、言葉というのは、非常に大事です。私は、そう思います。

2　侵略の危機が近づいている日本

大発展してきた「幸福の科学」

　幸福の科学を設立してより26年間（説法当時）、私は多くのことを経験してきました。

　現在、日本には、支部精舎と支部・拠点が500以上あり、世界にも、ほぼ100カ国に、私たちの

Power to the Future

宗教活動の拠点があります。また、正心館（当会の研修施設）も数多くあり、日本には25カ所以上あります。

それに加え、私たちは、すでに2年以上前に幸福の科学学園をスタートさせ、現在では、次の幸福の科学学園の開校も予定しています。2つ目の学園は、関西での中高一貫校となります（2013年4月に開校）。

そして、来る2015年には、幸福の科学学園の大学バージョン、つまり幸福の科学大学を千葉県に開学することを計画しています。

「近未来の恐怖」を警告した二つの映画

そして、今まさに、この瞬間、この6月に、日本全国200カ所以上において、私たちは、最新の映画「ファイナル・ジャッジメント」を観ること

ができます（説法当時）。

　この映画は実写であり、俳優や女優が、近未来の日本における、宗教の抵抗運動の話を演じています。

　これは一種の予言映画です。もちろん、ＳＦ（サイエンスフィクション）の類ではありますが、実際に、現実の国際政治の観点から見れば、見当違いの話でも、想像上の物語でもありません。それは、起こりうる可能性のあることなのです。

　さらに、この秋には、次の映画「神秘の法」が上映されます。

　今年（2012年）は、2本の映画がありますが、両方とも、日本の人々に、そして、もちろん、日本を取り巻く外国の人々にも、「近い将来、重大かつ巨大な兆しが現れてくる」と訴えています。それは、侵略する力であり、拡大する力です。日本

Power to the Future

に危険が切迫していることは間違いないのです。私は、そう考えます。

したがって、私たちは、近未来に起こりうる困難や恐怖について告げているのです。私たちは、それに備えなければなりません。

これは、日本の政治家が言うべきことです。当然、トップか、高い立場にある政治家の誰かが、そのような脅威があること、つまり、「日本に恐怖をもたらす国々がある」ということを言明すべきなのです。

しかし、日本には、そのような恐怖があることについて語れる政治家は、あまりいません。

そこで、私たちは宗教勢力であり、私は宗教家であるのですが、あえて、「もうすぐ危機が来るから、それに備えなければならない」と告げているわけです。

Be Strong

日本は守るべき「美しい国」

日本は、今、大きな力を持っています。少なくとも、経済力においてはそうです。

しかしながら、日本は、国際政治、すなわち外交においては、十分な力を持っていません。というのも、自国の近現代史に対して自信が欠けているからです。

日本の政治家は、ときどき、第二次世界大戦に関して、アジアの他の国々に謝罪の意を示すことがあります。しかし、彼らは、迫りくる日本の危機については、人々を目覚めさせていないのです。

もし、日本が数十年前に悪いことをしたとしても、現在、ほかの国が、かつての日本のようなことをするのであれば、逆に、私たち日本人は、自分たちで自国を守るために備えなければなりませ

Power to the Future

ん。なぜなら、私は日本を愛しているからです。

　日本は美しい国であり、伝統的・文化的な長い歴史を持っています。それは世界の遺産です。それを、この世から消滅させてはならないのです。

　私たちは、他の国々の魔の手から、守らなければなりません。この「守る」ということには、アジアの他の小さな国々の防衛をも含まれていると思います。

3 「正義」についての基準を持て

「遺憾です」という言い訳は許されない

　私はあえて申し上げます。

　歴史は歴史です。歴史を書く人には、正しいところも間違っているところもあるはずです。しかし、世界の歴史は、すべて、勝利を収めた人々に

Be Strong

よって書かれてきたのです。

　そのため、「歴史の記述が正しいか、正しくないか」ということは、正義の観点からではなく、勝利の観点から決定されています。

　これが歴史における真実です。歴史は歴史です。

　しかし、この時代、私たちは、「正義についての基準」を持たなければなりません。日本人は、「善と悪」「神と邪悪」に関する基準を持つだけの強さを持たなければならないと私は考えます。

　一切(いっさい)の言い訳は許されません。日本の政治家は、ときおり、上手に言い訳をします。それは、映画「ファイナル・ジャッジメント」でも描かれていました。彼らがいつも言うのは、「まことに遺憾(いかん)です」ということです。それしか言いません。

　ただ、「それについては遺憾です」「その状態については遺憾です」「その世界的な出来事の発生に

ついては遺憾です」と言っても、それには、ほとんど何の意味もないのです。

私たちは、善悪を分ける何らかの視点、立脚点を持たなければなりません。

「神から祝福されている国」の見分け方

もし、人々が幸福に、自由に、豊かに生活している国があるなら、そのような国は、それ自体、善であり、神の力によって導かれているはずだと私は思います。

そして、もし、その自由が神によって祝福されているのであれば、そのような国は、未来に向けて存続されるべきであると考えます。

一方、悪い国があって、その国の政府や当局が、人々を抑圧したり、人々が抗議することを許さなかったり、「言論の自由」「出版の自由」「信教の自

Be Strong

由」「良心の自由」を持つことを許さなかったりするのであれば、そのような国は、神や仏から祝福されていません。

　私たちは、「どちらが善で、どちらが悪か」「どちらが真実で、どちらが偽りか」「どちらが神に愛されることで、どちらが神に嫌われることか」ということについて、心を決めるべきなのです。

日本人には「新しい独立記念日」が必要

　私たち日本人は、「日本は独立国である」ということを宣言しなければなりません。私たちには、「新たな独立記念日」が必要なのです。

　67年以上前、日本人は第二次世界大戦での敗戦を経験しました。その後、独立を果たしましたが、私たちは、アメリカ合衆国に頼りすぎてきています。まさに、善悪を決めるすべての権限を譲って

Power to the Future

しまっています。そのほとんどすべては、アメリカ合衆国に譲り渡されているのです。

しかし、アメリカはアメリカです。合衆国は合衆国です。日本は日本です。日本は、自分たちで、自分たちのために、自主防衛について決断しなければなりません。

そこで、私たちは、最近の危機についての意見として、平和的な"武器"を解き放ちました。それが、映画「ファイナル・ジャッジメント」の主な内容です。

「平和主義」だけでは国が滅びる

宗教家として、私が申し上げたいのは、次のようなことです。

仏教の歴史では、ほとんどの仏教徒が、平和的であり、平和主義者でした。仏教徒のほとんどは、

Be Strong

政治的な意味においても、平和主義者だったのです。

しかし、今日、例えば、旧ビルマ、つまり現在のミャンマーでは、イスラム勢力と仏教勢力の間に紛争があり、仏教勢力でさえ自衛力を持っています。すなわち、軍隊を持っているのです。そうしなければ、彼らは、簡単にイスラム勢力に滅ぼされてしまうでしょう。この世で正義を実現する力がなくなるからです。

かつて、2500年以上前、私はネパールに生まれ、インドで活動をしました。当時、仏陀として私が常にみなさんに教えていたのは、「平和主義」と「心の平和」ということです。

私は、敵の侵略や国の滅亡が好きではありませんでしたが、例えば、生まれ故郷の釈迦国は、近隣の大国に滅ぼされてしまいました。これは、た

Power to the Future

いへん悲しいことです。釈迦国の人々は、仏教の熱心な信者だったので、そのとき、抵抗(ていこう)することもなく、滅ぼされてしまったのです。

　この伝統は、2000年以上にわたり、仏教の根底に流れ続けています。

新しい「平和と正義の哲学(てつがく)」が求められている

　しかし、今、私はあえて申し上げます。

　仏教には、世界平和の観点からの正義が必要です。それは、実際には、国連の正義であるべきなのです。

　もし、国連がうまく機能すれば、彼らの正義が世界中に平和をつくり出すでしょうが、現在、国連は機能していません。ですから、世界は、「平和と正義」に関する新しい哲学(てつがく)を求めているのです。

　あえて申し上げますが、それは、幸福の科学に

かかっています。私が善悪を峻別(しゅんべつ)していきましょう。私には、そのような力があるのです。

4　責任を取れる「強い人」となれ

「大きな力」には「大きな責任」が伴(ともな)う

　また、私は、「大きな力には、大きな責任が伴(ともな)う」と考えています。

　つまり、もし、あなたが大きな力を持っているならば、あなたには、通常あるいは必然的に、大きな責任が伴うのです。

　日本や日本人は、今、世界で大きな力を持っていますが、この大きな力には、大きな責任が伴います。ここで言う「come(カム)」とは、責任が「生じる」「伴う」という意味です。

　ですから、私は、日本の政治家や、これから政

治家になる人に対して、「今、あなたがたは、世界で大きな力を持っているのだ」ということを言いたいのです。

　この国は、大きな力を持っています。この国は、欧州連合(おうしゅう)の経済危機を救うことができますし、アメリカと良好な関係を保ち続ければ、近い将来、平和な世界をつくることもできるのです。

　繰(く)り返しますが、私たちには大きな力があります。それは、「大きな責任を伴う」ということを意味しているのです。

強い人とは「責任を取れる人」のこと

　日本においては、「責任」ということが非常に重要です。

　「責任を持つ」ということは、「あなたは弱くない」ということを意味しています。あなたは、弱

Be Strong

い人間ではありません。あなたがたは、弱い人々ではありません。

　責任を取れる人々とは、強い人々のことです。個々人で言えば、もし責任を取れるのなら、あなたは、強い男性、強い女性であるのです。

　強くなりたければ、責任を取ってください。

「自信」「日々の努力」「強い志」が必要

　どうすれば、責任を取れるのでしょうか。これが次の問題です。確かに、みなさんは、このような疑問を持つに違いありません。

　あなたがたの責任は、あなたがたの「自信」「日々の努力」「強い志」からつくられるのです。

　私、大川隆法は、外見的には普通の人間です。しかし、私は、志において強いのです。これが違いです。私には、強い志があります。「世界を、よ

Power to the Future

り幸福に、より平和にしたい」という強い意志があります。こうした意志が、あなたがたにも必要なのです。

　これよりのち、あなたがたは、次のことについて考えてください。それは、「大きな力には、大きな責任が伴う。大きな責任は、あなたがたの『志』から生まれてくる」ということです。

　日本では、最近、「心が折れる」と言われることがあります。これは、「失恋（しつれん）」ではなく、「志を捨てる」という意味です。しかし、それは、よいことではありません。

　よき習慣を身につけることにおいて、日々、怠（なま）けることなく、建設的であってください。そして、自らの意志で決断をしてください。それが、あなたがたにとっての「新しい力」となるでしょう。

　この決断が、自らの進路に関して責任を取るこ

Be Strong

とが、「未来に向けての新しい力」となるのです。
私は、そう考えます。

Chapter Two

Love and Justice
（愛と正義）

Lecture Given in English on October 6, 2012
at Master's Holy Temple: Sacred Shrine of Great Enlightenment, Taigokan
Happy Science, Tokyo

（2012年10月6日　東京都・幸福の科学 教祖殿 大悟館にて）

1 Justice: An Urgent Matter for the Japanese

Today is a memorial day for Happy Science. It is the 26th anniversary of the establishment of our group and, in addition to that, the premiere of our new animation movie, *The Mystical Laws.**

Today's theme is "Love and Justice." This is a new theme for us and it is not so easy.

I have already taught a lot about love. For example, you already know about the Fourfold Path: love, wisdom, self-reflection, and progress. These are very important teachings in our group.

You also have already heard that love is forgiveness; love is mercy; love is to give something to another person and not to take from others.

* Dates and titles are at the time of the lecture.

Love and Justice

But now, we have another problem, and that is justice. This is an urgent problem for the Japanese people right now.

2 Japan's Confidence Shaken by the Takeshima and Senkaku Islands Issues

Xi Jinping aims to expand his "empire"

Currently in Japan, Happy Science and the Happiness Realization Party are fighting against invading powers.

This is expressed in our new movie, *The Mystical Laws*. The Godom Empire is a fictional country, but there is a model for it, of course. It is China and its next "emperor," Xi Jinping.

They aim to expand their "empire" and are

causing a lot of trouble around Asia, in the territorial sea of the Philippines and Vietnam for example, and of course that of Japan.

South Korea controls Takeshima as a symbol of its independence

Japan has had two major issues since August 2012.

One is Takeshima Islands in Shimane Prefecture, Japan. It is called Dokdo in South Korea. In reality, South Korea has been controlling these islands for several decades, ever since they set up the Yi Seungman Line, in 1952, after World War II. At that time, Japan did not have the Self-Defense Force, so the Japanese people could not do anything about it. After setting up the Yi Seungman Line, in that same year, President

Love and Justice

Yi Seungman declared that Takeshima Islands belonged to South Korea.

An alliance between America and Japan was formed by the San Francisco Peace Treaty in 1951, and at that time, the United States of America, of course, thought that Takeshima Islands belonged to Japan.

But Korean people are taught by their government that Takeshima is Dokdo and that it belongs to South Korea. Also, they are taught that the islands were occupied by Japan in 1905 before Korea was merged into Japan in 1910. The Korean government says that this was the first step of intrusion by Japan.

Yet, in Japanese history, there is no historical evidence to prove that. Takeshima belonged to

Japan before the Edo period (1603~1868), but no one occupied it in those times. The argument is very urgent and fierce so it is a very difficult issue now. South Korea will never give up its occupation of Takeshima because it is a symbol of South Korea's independence.

The reason behind China's allegation of its authority over Senkaku Islands

Another issue is Senkaku Islands, also known as the Senkaku islets because it is a group of small islands.

It has now become a major problem because China has sent a lot of its government vessels around these islands for surveillance. China is saying that Senkaku Islands belong to China.

However, Japanese people lived on Senkaku Islands since the 19th century and established fishing industries, or caught birds to make beautiful feathers that go on top of ladies' hats. There were Japanese people on these islands. About ninety years ago, or in 1920, the Republic of China sent a letter of thanks to the Senkaku people for rescuing the Chinese people. So China also agreed that Senkaku belonged to Japan.

Yet, in 1968, there was the discovery of an abundance of crude oil below the bottom of the Japanese territorial waters surrounding Senkaku Islands. So, unfortunately, China suddenly changed its attitude and, since 1970, argued that Senkaku Islands originally belonged to China.

The Japanese people do not agree with China

on this matter. In fact, the Japan Coast Guard has protected this area as the territory of Japan for more than forty years. That is why Prime Minister Yoshihiko Noda said that the islands belong to Japan and we will not give that power or right to China.

China became more aggressive in response to Japan's nationalization of Senkaku Islands
Senkaku Islands originally belonged to a private Japanese owner and Japan bought the rights to these islands, in September 2012, as national property in order to protect the islands from Chinese, and sometimes Taiwanese, intrusion.

Prior to this bargaining period there was a dispute between Tokyo Governor Shintaro Ishihara

Love and Justice

and Prime Minister Noda. Governor Ishihara of Tokyo wanted to buy Senkaku Islands because if the Japanese government bought these islets, the government would do nothing about it. "Nothing" means the government would prohibit Japanese people from entering the islands, from building some kind of facility or from taking other actions to provoke the Chinese government.

Prime Minister Noda, however, negotiated with the owner and finally won the rights over the property. Following that, the Chinese government vessels have been sailing around Senkaku Islands.

As some of you may know, this matter was in dispute in the United Nations last month (Sep. 2012). Prime Minister Noda made a speech about

Senkaku Islands without pointing out the names of other countries, to the effect of saying we will not abandon our sovereignty over the islands. A representative of the Chinese Ministry of Foreign Affairs, however, stated seven times that Japan stole the islands. It was a very infuriating argument and we were astonished by those words.

Takeshima and Senkaku Islands: a struggle of the balance of power in Asia

The above two issues will not be solved easily because there is a struggle in the balance of power between large Asian countries, Japan and China. These two giant countries are actually rivals in the field of economy. South Korea, too, is attacking Japan's economy. So these problems are very difficult to solve. These issues include matters of economic profits and also, in the political meaning, the sovereignty over the islands.

Furthermore, if the people who are in charge of this matter have power, they can cause a dispute or conflict, or even start a war.

The United States of America is now voicing their thoughts about this matter. For example, it declares that the Senkaku Islands are protected under Article 5 of the Japan-U.S. Security Treaty which declares that if an allied country is intruded or attacked by another country, then the United States of America will fight together with Japan. The U.S. Defense Secretary clearly stated this.

3 The Happiness Realization Party Has Been Claiming the Need for National Defense

So we, the Happiness Realization Party, have been making a movement all over Japan regarding the necessity of self-defense.

When our party was formed three years ago, the self-defense issue was regarded as a very minor argument. The two dominant parties in Japan, namely the Liberal Democratic Party and the Democratic Party of Japan, did not mention the self-defense of Japan and the urgency of it during the general election in 2009. But our party insisted that it was very important and that foreign affairs would be the main point in

Love and Justice

the next three or four years.

Our prediction was correct and now the thoughts of the Japanese people are changing. Recently, there was an election within the LDP. There were five candidates and they all said that focusing on self-defense is essential.

Prime Minister Noda, the third prime minister of the Democratic Party of Japan, also bent the direction of their party and says almost the same thing as the conservative parties.

So almost all the parties in Japan are now thinking that self-defense is very important, just as we predicted three and a half years ago.

4 The Danger of Losing Senkaku Islands

China will surely set up missile facilities on Senkaku Islands

In the midst of the recent disputes and confrontations, whether these two conflicts – the one between Japan and South Korea, and the other between Japan and China – lead to a war or not is very difficult to understand and argue. Despite that, some left-wing supporters easily say, "Please abandon the sovereignty over the islands. It will lead to friendships between Japan and other countries. We can be friends from now on." People of religious nature are apt to say these kinds of things. They easily

Love and Justice

surrender and abandon their rights.

But in this context, what would happen if the Chinese government occupies Senkaku Islands? Although the Senkaku Islands are small islets, they are very close to Taiwan.

The Chinese government wants to take Taiwan within these several years, but the Taiwanese Army is very strong, so if the U.S. forces assist Taiwan, China will be unable to conquer Taiwan. Also, Japan has the Self-Defense Force. If the Japanese attitude changes and a collective defense system by these two countries can function properly, it will be very difficult for China.

If the Chinese government succeeds in occupying Senkaku Islands, China will surely,

I would even say definitely, set up missile facilities on these small islands. These missile facilities would of course be capable of launching missiles at Taiwan, Okinawa, as well as at South Korea, mainland Japan, the Philippines and other Asian countries. So, although Senkaku Islands are small islands, the Japanese government cannot abandon its sovereignty over them.

Japan's SLOC under threat means no crude oil for Japan

All Japan can do is just to protect its right over these islands. Japan is prohibited, by Article 9 of the Japanese Constitution, from settling the diplomatic conflicts through war and invasion

Love and Justice

of other countries. Hence, the Japanese people can do nothing but assert their rights.

On the contrary, China can do anything. This Senkaku Islands matter is not a small issue. China could possibly take a stance toward solving energy problems, of course, by taking control of these islets. But its military strategy is planned out much further. A virtual war between two great countries, China and the United States of America, is what they are really thinking about.

Thus, although this problem may seem small, it is a great matter in the long run.

If we lose our rights over Senkaku Islands and China invades Taiwan, we will be unable to get crude oil via supertankers coming in from the west, from Arabic countries. This means that we will not be able to produce electricity from thermal power using oil.

5 Why Japan Must Preserve Nuclear Power Plants

Real cause of the Fukushima NPP accident: breakdown of emergency cooling generators

There is another crisis in Japan.

We experienced a great disaster in the eastern part of Japan in 2011 which led to the Fukushima Daiichi Nuclear Power Plant (NPP) problem. There was an accident at the Fukushima Daiichi NPP and as a result, an anti-nuclear power movement has been prevailing.

Love and Justice

The Happiness Realization Party is the only party insisting that nuclear power plants are very important. The accident at the Fukushima Daiichi NPP was miserable for the Japanese people, but there were no deaths caused by that accident.

This accident was caused by the great tsunami resulting from the enormous, magnitude 9.0-grade earthquake. It is said to occur once in 600 years. That is the length of time between these great earthquakes.

The real cause of this accident was the breakdown of emergency electric generators designed to automatically cool the nuclear reactors. The electric generators were damaged by the powerful waves of the tsunami. That is the sad truth of this accident. In short, the problem was not in the nuclear reactors themselves.

European and American people, or people of other countries, misunderstand this fact. The problem was not in the nuclear reactor or nuclear power facilities. It was simply the generators. A small problem, that's all.

If these facilities were set up higher than twenty meters above ground, there would have been no such accident. It was not the nuclear facilities' fault.

The Japanese designers thought about this at first. They originally designed the nuclear power plant at a higher position, more than thirty-five meters above sea level.

But an American engineer advised that it was

not necessary, and that just ten meters was enough. So the hill was razed to make a flat surface, and that is where the Fukushima Daiichi NPP was constructed. That was the reason.

In order to solve the energy problem, we should not act based on emotions

We need electric power for industries and for the protection of our daily lives. We also have the sea lane dilemma where crude oil from the south and the west could be attacked by China or other countries. So, we cannot depend on thermal power alone.

We courageously insist that we keep our nuclear power. Electricity bills in the residential sectors have gone up since September 2012. We, the Japanese people, can only supply four percent of the energy by ourselves.

The energy problem is very complex but also very important, so we should not act solely based on emotions.

We have already experienced two atomic bombs in 1945, one in Hiroshima and the other in Nagasaki. So, people are apt to hate the word *nuclear* or *radiation*. Even so, atomic bombs and nuclear power plants are different. It depends on how we use that power.

6 Japan Must Debate More Strongly Against Foreign Countries

China and North Korea's possession of nuclear missiles allows them to threaten Japan

Additionally, Japan is surrounded by militarized countries, such as China, which already possess nuclear missiles.

North Korea is almost done developing its nuclear missiles as well. It sometimes threatens Japan. North Korea is a small country that does not have enough food for its own people, but it can threaten Japan. The same goes for China.

China has nuclear weapons, so they are threatening Japan this time regarding Senkaku Islands.

They were most likely authorized to demonstrate and attacked the official vehicle of the Japanese ambassador. They attacked Japanese enterprises and Japanese department stores, and stole a lot of goods.

Yet there was no apology for all that. They just say Japan did a terrible thing to them during the last war.

"200,000 comfort women" is impossible

It is the same for South Korea. Korean people say, "Japan employed comfort women by using military power, and produced more than 200,000 comfort women from Korea." This is too large a number. It is impossible! That is almost the size of the military. 200,000 comfort women? How could we have sent them to some small islands in the southern part of Asia? We did not even have enough food at the time. It is impossible. The number is way too large.

Unfortunately, U.S. Secretary of State Hillary Clinton misunderstood and thought that comfort women meant sex slaves. That is a terrible misunderstanding and a misconception.

South Korea took advantage of this misunderstanding, and made a statue of a thirteen year-old little girl, a comfort girl, just across the road in front of the Japanese embassy. Koreans are saying that they will build this kind of statue of a comfort woman, a statue of a little girl, in New Jersey, New York and other places. They are making some kind of joint anti-Japanese promotion with the government and private sectors.

The Koreans and the Chinese like to debate, but the Japanese do not

In the background lies a Japanese cultural tradition that the Japanese people do not voice enough things about their past. They sometimes remain silent about the past. In Japan, there is a tradition that, when its army is defeated, the head of the army should say nothing about it. No excuse is allowed in Japan. That is why the Japanese people have not said anything regarding their own deeds.

The Korean and Chinese people, on the other hand, like to debate. They are almost European or American. They need to debate.

They usually go overboard because they are just waiting for a rebuttal against their argument. So, the Japanese people must debate more strongly. I believe so.

7 Establish Justice by the Power of Wisdom

To stop evil deeds is an act of good and an act of justice

Going back to the first topic of love and justice, love is essential and to love others is truly wonderful. To love thy neighbor is quite a difficult task, but it is very important and, historically speaking, it is an order from God.

We also think, however, that justice is just as

critical. There are approximately 200 countries in the world, and a lot of conflicts occur between several countries. Sometimes these conflicts lead to war. At such times, the decision of right and wrong should be made from the universal perspective. That is when we need justice. The point is, love is important, but wisdom is required to consider what kind of love you should give to other people. If there are many evil deeds occurring due to influences by evil spirits, then such acts must be stopped. To stop evil deeds is good. That is justice.

Think of love from the viewpoint of wisdom

We are seeking wisdom. We must think of love from the viewpoint of wisdom. We need

Love and Justice

wisdom, especially in a relationship between two countries.

Syria, for example, is experiencing a civil war and more than 30,000 people have been killed by government forces. More than 30,000 civilians were killed.[†]

In such times, some great countries must speak out and stop the civil war. I believe that is the right thing to do.

It is, however, incredibly challenging. Every country has its own issue, and it has its own reasons, so it's very difficult.

Despite that, we must seek for what is right and we must establish justice by dint of wisdom. We must think about what love is in this context. "The love for many people" and "the love on

---

[†] Estimated number of deaths at the time of the lecture. According to the U.N., the estimated number of deaths is 70,000 people as of March 2013.

a personal level" are slightly different from each other. No, they are very different.

If a country is destroyed by a lack of wisdom, then that is not love. If an ill-willed country intrudes other countries due to a lack of wisdom and many people suffer from such an invasion, then that is evil.

At such a time, the United Nations or other great powers should stop those evil deeds. That is justice. We usually think of love as something personal, but concerning international politics we must seek for justice in terms of wisdom when it comes to conflicts between countries or civil wars. So, in this lecture, I added justice to love and wisdom.

Love and Justice

（和訳）第2章　愛と正義

1　日本人にとって緊急を要する「正義」の問題

　今日（10月6日）は、幸福の科学にとっての記念日です。立宗満26周年記念日に加え、今日は、私たちの最新のアニメ映画「神秘の法」の公開初日です（説法当時）。

　さて、今日のテーマは「愛と正義」です。これは、それほど簡単なものではなく、かつ、私たちにとっては新しいテーマです。

　私は、すでに、愛に関して数多くの教えを説いています。例えば、愛・知・反省・発展の四正道については、みなさんもすでにご存じでしょう。これらは、当会では非常に重要な教えです。

Power to the Future

　また、みなさんは、「愛とは許しである」「愛とは慈悲である」「愛とは、他の人に何かを与えることであり、他の人から奪うことではない」という教えも聞いたことがあるでしょう。

　しかし、今や、私たちは別の問題を抱えています。それは「正義」の問題です。これは、今、日本人にとって緊急を要する問題なのです。

2　「竹島・尖閣問題」で揺れる日本

"帝国"の拡大を目論む習近平

　今、日本で、私たち、つまり幸福の科学と幸福実現党は侵略勢力と戦っています。

　それは、最新の映画「神秘の法」でも描かれています。映画に出てくるゴドム帝国というのは、架空の話ですが、もちろん、それにはモデルがあ

Love and Justice

ります。それは、中国であり、次の"皇帝"の習近平です。

　彼らは、自らの"帝国"を拡大しようと目論んでおり、アジア地域で数多くのトラブルを起こしています。それは、例えば、フィリピンやベトナムの領海、そして、もちろん、日本の領海におけるトラブルです。

「独立の象徴」として竹島を実効支配する韓国

　日本は、2012年8月から、二つの大きな問題を抱えています。

　一つは、日本の島根県にある「竹島」です。韓国では、独島と呼ばれています。

　この島は、第二次大戦後、1952年に、李承晩ラインを設定して以来、数十年にわたり、韓国が実効支配しています。当時、日本には自衛隊がなかっ

Power to the Future

たため、日本人はどうすることもできませんでした。その年、李承晩大統領は、「竹島は韓国に属する」と宣言したのです。

　日本が日米同盟およびサンフランシスコ平和条約を結んだ1951年当時、アメリカ合衆国は、もちろん、「竹島は日本に属する」と考えていました。

　しかし、韓国の人々は、政府から、「竹島は、独島であり、韓国に属している。1910年に韓国が日本に併合される前、1905年に日本に占領されたのだ」と教えられています。韓国政府は、「それが日本による侵略の第一歩だった」と主張しているのです。

　ただ、日本の歴史には、それを証明する史実はありません。竹島は、江戸時代（1603～1868）から日本に属しており、当時、島には誰も住んでいなかったのです。

Love and Justice

　この議論は、非常に緊迫しており、かつ、激しいものであるため、今、非常に難しい問題となっています。

　韓国は、竹島の占拠を決してあきらめないでしょう。なぜなら、竹島は、韓国の「独立の象徴」だからです。

中国が「尖閣の領有権」を主張し始めた理由

　もう一つの問題は、尖閣諸島（Senkaku Islands）です。小さな島々なので、尖閣諸島（Senkaku islets）とも言います。

　ここは、今、非常に大きな問題となっています。なぜなら、中国が、尖閣諸島の監視のために数多くの公船を送り、「尖閣諸島も中国に属する」と主張しているからです。

　しかし、尖閣諸島には、19世紀から日本人が住

み、漁業をしたり、婦人帽のてっぺんに付ける美しい羽をつくるために鳥を捕獲したりしていました。そこには日本人が住んでいたのです。

　また、約90年前の1920年、中華民国は、中国人を救助した尖閣の人々に感謝状を送っています。そのように、当時の中国も、尖閣諸島は日本に属していることを認めていたのです。

　ところが、1968年、尖閣諸島周辺の日本の領海の海底に大量の石油が眠っていることが発見されると、残念なことに、中国は、突然、態度を変えました。そして、1970年以降、「尖閣諸島はもともと中国のものだ」と主張し始めたのです。

　日本人は、それについては合意しておらず、実際、日本の海上保安庁が、この海域を40年以上にわたって日本の領海として支配しています。

　それで、野田佳彦首相（当時）も、「尖閣諸島は

Love and Justice

日本に属しており、その権限や権利は中国には渡さない」と言っているのです。

尖閣国有化を機に激しくなった「中国の反応」

　尖閣諸島は、もともと、日本人が個人で所有していましたが、中国の侵入や、ときどきある台湾の侵入から守るために、2012年9月、日本政府が、その所有権を買い取り、国有化しました。

　この売買交渉が行われる前、石原慎太郎都知事（当時）と野田首相との間で論争がありました。石原都知事は、尖閣諸島を購入したがっていました。というのも、彼は、「日本政府が尖閣諸島を購入したら、日本政府は何もしないだろう。すなわち、政府は、日本人が尖閣諸島に上陸したり、何らかの施設を建設したり、その他、中国政府を刺激するような行動を起こすことを禁じるだろう」と考

Power to the Future

えたからです。

　しかし、野田首相は、島の所有者と交渉し、最終的に、その所有権を獲得しました。その後、中国公船が、尖閣諸島周辺を徘徊するようになっているのです。

　ご存じの人もいらっしゃるでしょうが、先月(2012年9月)、国連で議論がなされました。野田首相は、他国の名前を出さずに演説をし、「島の領有権を放棄しない」という趣旨のことを訴えました。

　それに対して、中国外務省の代表者は、「日本は尖閣諸島を盗んだ」と、7回も主張したのです。その怒り狂った主張に、私たちはたいへん驚きました。

Love and Justice

「竹島・尖閣」はアジアのパワーバランスの問題

　この二つの問題は、簡単には解決しないでしょう。これは、日本と中国という、アジアの大国のパワーバランス（力の均衡）の問題だからです。この二つの大国は、経済力において、実際にはライバルです。そして、韓国も、日本に経済的な攻勢をかけています。

　ですから、これらの問題の解決は、非常に難しいのです。経済的な利益がかかっている上に、政治的には、島の領有権がかかっているからです。

　この問題に対して権限を持つ人々は、論争や対立を起こすことも、戦争を起こすことも可能です。

　そして今、アメリカ合衆国は、この問題について声明を出しています。例えば、「尖閣諸島は日米安全保障条約第５条の適用の対象であり、同盟国が、他国に侵略あるいは攻撃された場合、アメリ

カ合衆国は日本とともに戦う」と宣言しています。国防長官が、それを明言しているのです。

3 「国防」を訴え続けている幸福実現党

　幸福実現党は、日本全国で、国防の必要性を訴える運動をしてきています。

　3年前（2009年）に私たちが立党したころ、この問題は、それほど大きく取り上げられませんでした。2009年の総選挙では、日本の主要政党、つまり、自民党と民主党という二大政党は、国防の緊急性について触れなかったのです。

　しかし、私たちの政党は、「国防は非常に重要である。ここ3～4年の間に、外交問題が主要な論点になる」と訴えていたのです。

　私たちの予想は正しく、今、日本人の考えは変

Love and Justice

わってきています。最近、自民党の総裁選がありましたが（説法当時）、5人の候補者は、みな、「国防を重視することが不可欠である」と主張していました。

また、野田首相は、民主党3代目の首相ですが、彼もまた、自らの党の方針を曲げ、保守政党とほとんど変わらないことを言うようになっています。

3年半前に私たちが予言したように、今や、日本のほとんどの政党は、「国防は極めて重要なものである」と考えているのです。

4 尖閣を失うことの危険性

中国は尖閣に「ミサイル施設」をつくるはず

さて、この論争や対立の最中にあって、「韓国や中国との間にあるこれら二つの対立が、戦争に発

93

展していくかどうか」について理解し、議論するのは、非常に難しいことです。

しかし、左翼系の人々は、いとも簡単に、「島の領有権は放棄したほうがよい。そうすれば、日本は、他国と友好関係を築けて、今後、仲良くできる」と言います。そのような人々は、宗教的な人に多いのですが、彼らは、簡単に降参し、権利を放棄するのです。

ただ、その場合、例えば、尖閣諸島について言えば、もし、中国政府が尖閣諸島を占領したならば、どうなるでしょうか。尖閣諸島は、小さな島々とはいえ、台湾に非常に近いのです。

中国政府は、ここ数年の間に台湾を取りたいわけですが、台湾軍は非常に強く、もし米軍が彼らを支援すれば、中国は台湾を征服することができません。また、日本にも自衛隊があります。もし、

Love and Justice

日本の態度が変わり、2カ国による集団的自衛体制が機能すれば、中国にとっては非常に難しくなります。

　一方、もし、中国政府が尖閣諸島を占領することに成功したならば、彼らは、間違いなく、この小さな島々にミサイル施設をつくるでしょう。

　このミサイル施設からは、もちろん台湾や沖縄に向けて発射可能ですし、韓国、日本本土、フィリピン、そして、他のアジアの国々に向けても発射可能です。

　したがって、たとえ小さな島といえども、日本政府は、その領有権を放棄することができないのです。

シーレーンが脅かされ、石油が入らなくなる

　日本は、自らの権利を守る以上のことは、何も

できません。つまり、日本国憲法第9条によって、他の国々に侵攻し、戦争によって外交問題を解決することが禁じられているのです。

そのため、日本人は、ほとんど何もできません。単に、自らの権利を主張するだけです。

一方、中国人は何でもできるのです。

この尖閣諸島は小さな問題ではありません。

もちろん、中国は、「これらの島々の獲得を通じて、エネルギー問題を解決する」という姿勢を取ることも可能でしょうが、彼らの軍事戦略はもっと先を行っています。彼らは、二つの大国による仮想戦争、すなわち、中国とアメリカ合衆国との仮想戦争を考えているのです。

ですから、この問題は小さいように見えますが、長い目で見れば、重大な問題なのです。

もし、私たち日本人が尖閣諸島の領有権を失い、

Love and Justice

中国が台湾を侵略したならば、どうなるでしょうか。日本は、西のアラブ諸国から巨大タンカーによって原油を輸入していますが、それが手に入らなくなります。

それは、私たちが、石油を使用する火力発電から電気を得られなくなることを意味しているのです。

5　日本が「原発」を維持すべき理由

事故の本当の原因は「冷却用電源の喪失」

日本には、もう一つの危機があります。

2011年、東日本で大きな災害が起き、福島第一原発の問題が発生しました。福島第一原発の施設が事故を起こし、日本で、反原発運動が盛んになっているのです。

幸福実現党だけが、「原発は非常に重要である」

と主張しています。

　日本人にとって、福島第一原発の事故は悲惨なものでしたが、原発事故による死者は一人も出ていません。それは、巨大な津波による事故だったのです。

　マグニチュード9.0の巨大地震が起きたわけですが、それは「600年に一度」とも言われるものでした。今回のような巨大地震は、そのような長い周期でしか起こらないのです。

　そして、今回の事故の本当の原因は、原子炉冷却用のポンプを動かすための緊急用発電機の故障にありました。その発電機が、大津波によって壊れてしまったのです。それは悲しい事故でした。

　要するに、原子炉そのものの問題ではなかったのです。欧米や他の国の人々は、それについて誤解しています。原発事故は、原子炉や原発施設の

Love and Justice

問題ではなかったのです。単なる発電機の問題であり、それは小さな問題だったのです。それだけだったわけです。

　もし、この施設を 20 メートル以上高い所につくっていたら、そのような事故は起こらなかったはずです。ですから、原発施設の欠陥のせいではないのです。

　当初、日本の設計者も、それについて考えていました。彼らは、原発を、もっと高い場所、つまり、海抜 35 メートル以上の高台につくろうと計画していました。

　しかし、アメリカ人の技師が、「その必要はない。10 メートルの高さがあれば十分だ」とアドバイスしたので、丘を平らに削って、福島第一原発を建設したのです。それが理由です。

Power to the Future

エネルギー問題は「感情論」で動くべきではない

電力は、産業のためにも、日常生活の維持のためにも必要です。

さらに、日本には、シーレーン（海上交通路）の問題があります。つまり、南や西からの原油輸送は、中国やその他の国々によって攻撃されかねないため、私たちは、火力発電だけには頼れないのです。

したがって、私たちは、原子力発電を断固として維持することを主張しているのです。

2012年9月より、家庭向けの電気料金が通常より上がりました。また、私たち日本人は、たったの4パーセントしかエネルギーを自給できていません。

このように、エネルギー問題は、非常に難しいものですが、非常に重要でもあるので、感情論だ

Love and Justice

けで動くべきではありません。

　日本は、1945年に、広島と長崎に原爆を投下されているため、国民は、「核」あるいは「放射能」という言葉を嫌いがちです。しかし、「原爆」と「原発」は違います。それは使い方によるのです。

6　もっと強い姿勢で外国と討論を

「核」を背景に日本を脅してくる中国と北朝鮮

　それに加え、日本は、すでに、中国のような、核ミサイルを保有する軍事国家に囲まれています。

　北朝鮮も、核ミサイルをほぼ完成させており、彼らは、ときどき日本を威嚇します。北朝鮮は、国民の食料も十分にないほどの弱小国ですが、日本を脅すことができるのです。

　中国も同様です。中国は核兵器を持っているの

で、今回、尖閣諸島に関して、日本を脅しているのです。

　彼らは、おそらく公認と思われるデモを行いました。そして、日本大使の乗った公用車を襲撃し、日系企業や日系デパートを襲い、数多くの商品を略奪しました。

　しかし、それに対して何の謝罪もありません。彼らは、「日本は、先の戦争で悪いことをした」と言うだけなのです。

「20万人の従軍慰安婦」などありえない

　韓国も同じです。彼らは、「日本は、従軍慰安婦を使った。軍の命令で、朝鮮から20万人以上の女性が従軍慰安婦にされた」と言っています。しかし、これは、あまりにも多い人数です。ありえません！　それは、ほとんど軍隊と同じ人数です。

Love and Justice

　20万人もの従軍慰安婦を、アジアの南方の小さな島々に、どうやって輸送できるのでしょうか。当時は十分な食料もありませんでした。そんなことは不可能です。数が多すぎます。

　また、残念ながら、アメリカのヒラリー・クリントン国務長官（説法当時）は、従軍慰安婦を「性の奴隷」という意味に誤解しましたが、これは勘違いです。大いなる誤解なのです。

　しかし、韓国は、この誤解を利用しています。彼らは、13歳の少女の慰安婦像を、日本大使館の向かいの道路に設置しました。そして、「このような少女の慰安婦像を、ニュージャージーやニューヨーク、その他の場所にもつくる」と言っています。このように、政府と民間部門が一緒になって、反日運動を展開しているのです。

Power to the Future

日本人と違って討論を好む韓国人や中国人

　この背景には、「日本人は、自分たちの過去について十分に語らない」という文化的な伝統があります。日本人は、過去のことについては、今でも沈黙を守っています。

　日本には、「敗軍の将、兵を語らず」という伝統があり、言い訳は許されないのです。ですから、日本人は、自分たちの行為について、何も言わずにきたわけです。

　一方、韓国人や中国人は、討論を好む国民であり、欧米人とほとんど同じです。彼らは討論を必要としています。そして、彼らは、反論を期待しているため、たいてい言いすぎるのです。

　したがって、日本人は、もっともっと強い姿勢で討論すべきです。私はそう思います。

Love and Justice

7 「智慧の力」によって正義を確立せよ

悪行を止めることは「善」であり、「正義」

　最初の「愛と正義」の話に戻りますが、愛とは重要なものであり、他の人を愛するのは、とても素晴らしいことです。

　「隣人を愛する」というのは非常に難しいことですが、たいへん重要です。それは、歴史的に、「神の命令」なのです。

　一方、私たちは、「正義もまた非常に重要である」と考えています。

　世界には約200カ国があり、幾つかの国家間で、数多くの対立が起きています。それが、ときおり戦争に発展しています。

　その際には、「正しいか、間違っているか」ということを普遍的な観点から判断すべきです。そう

Power to the Future

いうときには正義が必要なのです。

　要するに、愛は大切ですが、「どのような愛を他の人々に与えるか」ということは、智慧をもって考慮すべきなのです。

　もし、悪霊の影響による悪事が数多く起きているならば、それを止めるべきです。悪行を止めることは善です。それは正義なのです。

「智慧の視点」から愛を考えよう

　私たちは智慧を求めています。智慧の視点から愛を考えるべきなのです。特に、二国間の関係においては、智慧が必要です。

　例えば、シリアでは、内戦状態が続いており、政府軍によって３万人以上の人々が殺されています。民間人が３万人以上も殺されているのです（注。説法当時の人数。国連によると、2013年3

Love and Justice

月時点で、死者は7万人に達すると推計される)。

　そのようなときは、大国が発言し、内戦を止めるべきです。それが正しいことだと私は思います。

　ただ、これは非常に難しいことです。どの国にも、固有の問題があり、それぞれに事情があるため、たいへん難しいのです。

　しかし、私たちは、「何が正しいのか」ということを探究し、「智慧の力」によって、正義を確立しなければなりません。そして、この意味において、「何が愛なのか」ということを考えるべきなのです。

　「多くの人々にとっての愛」と「個人的な愛」とは少し違います。いや、かなり違います。

　もし、智慧の不足によって、国が破壊されるならば、それは愛ではないと思います。

　また、智慧の不足によって、もし、悪しき国が他国を侵略し、多くの人々がその悪しき侵略によ

って苦しむのならば、それは悪です。

　そのときには、国連や他の大国が、その悪事を止めるべきなのです。それが正義です。

　私たちは、愛について、「個人的なもの」と考えがちですが、国際政治において、戦争や内戦が起きた場合には、智慧の視点から正義を求めなければなりません。

　今回の法話(ほうわ)では、私は、「愛と智慧」に「正義」を加えました。

Chapter Three

Power to the Future
（未来に力を）

Lecture Given in English on October 11, 2012
at Happy Science General Headquarters
Happy Science, Tokyo

（2012年10月11日　東京都・幸福の科学総合本部にて）

1 Three Hypotheses Regarding the Future of the World

Truly, truly, I'll say to you.

Today's lecture, "Power to the Future," is a great theme. It will decide our future destination. This future is the future of all nations in the world, including Japan.

We, the Japanese, are in adversity right now. This is just a turning point.

Some say that as China rises it will intrude on and swallow Japan. Although there are political and military powers working in the international community, China will overcome all of them and become the next controller of the world. This is one hypothesis.

Power to the Future

Another is that the United States of America will regain power. Allies of the United States will cooperate and protect themselves against the new emerging and intruding powers; the new imperial power of China, North Korea and so on. This is another story.

The third hypothesis concerns Japan only. We, Japanese people, should decide for ourselves and by ourselves, to stand on our own feet and protect the Asia and Oceania regions, and change the crisis into the peace and prosperity of the world. This is the third strategy.

I will now tell you about these.

2 Western Countries Take Economically Shrinking Policies

Japan still has potential for the future

I gave this lecture the title, "Power to the Future."

It means we need power to change our future. This power itself comes with the requirement to change the future, and the future, of course, will require more power from us than we used to have.

So, this means the word 'power' holds a lot of meanings.

For example, there is an IMF (International Monetary Fund) assembly going on in Japan now. More than 20,000 people from around the world attended.★

★ Dates and titles are at the time of the lecture.

It was to be held in Egypt, but Egypt is in the aftermath of mass demonstrations and is in a lot of confusion. Therefore, Japan took over this role in place of Egypt and invited many people from around the world.

Japan showed the people of the world that this is the style of the future and a new form of future. People who came from other Asian countries, South and Central America, Africa and Europe said, "Japan has potential. Japan still has potential for the future."

Japan in the 1990s: a learning material for the EU

What impressed me most on the first day was when an influential attendee at the IMF assembly, who is from Europe, commented, "We insisted that Japan's solution to its bad loan problem in the 1990s (injecting public funds into financial institutions) was not so good, but now we recognize that Japan did well. We, the people of Europe, must learn from Japan and catch up to your policy."

The world economy is now on the verge of decline. An example of this is, as the IMF announced yesterday, that the EU banks are scheduled to withdraw its loan amounts by about 350 trillion Japanese yen or so from all over the world. This is a huge amount.

Nonetheless it means that the EU banks is cutting its loan amount which therefore means reducing the loan amount to developing countries like

Africa, some parts of Asia, and other parts of the world. It means that the EU cannot fully conduct its duty.

That is why someone commented that since Japan is taking a strong yen policy and the Japanese yen has very much appreciated, Japan can save other parts of the world. I believe it's a very heavy burden, but also very important.

If the EU banks decide to concentrate on withdrawing its loans and clear its balance sheet, the EU banks will do better and better in the databases but the world economy will fall like Niagara Falls.

Obama does not have a sufficient economic policy
The subsequent issue is, of course, the U.S.

economy.

It's the presidential election period now, and a very close competition between Romney and Obama is in progress. However, they do not have a sufficient policy.

Obama wants to and will minimize the U.S. financial deficit, but on the other hand, Mitt Romney is going to change the government policy from a 'bigger government' to a 'smaller government.' This means the emergency economic policy is accompanied by a budget cut.

Romney may use more military budget than Obama, I guess, but he will surely aim to make a 'small government' policy. It's a traditional Republican way of thinking. So both the EU and the United States of America are taking a policy that aims to "shrink" their economy.

3 China is on the Verge of an Economic Debacle

China does not have enough financial knowledge and experience

A problem following that will be China.

This is just my guess, but China doesn't have enough financial knowledge and experience because it has only experienced an excessively high economic growth in these twenty years.

Prior to that, it was at a very, very primitive economic level, only at the level of a farming country, so this is the first time that it has found itself standing just before the cliff, or on the verge of an economic debacle.

This is China's first experience, so it will need to go through a lot of suffering. I think it will also face a lot of adversities because there is no such instance of a fall in economy in their history, at least in these last 100 years.

China should now learn from Japan. Japan can guide China on how to control its financial direction, but China will not hear anything from us. Thus, I believe China will miscontrol its way of handling the national economic policy.

What Japan needs in order to defend against Chinese invasion

China began facing this economic debacle in 2011. It is now 2012 and the problem is just growing bigger and bigger. Yet, China is not thinking too much about that. China is thinking that this is just one of the cycles, a cycle of economic downturn. It believes that, in the next one, two or three years, the economy will turn out to be good.

So China is throwing more money than usual into military power and wants to convert its military budget into the occupation, or threatening, of other countries to get their resources. By resources I mean crude oil, iron, and other metals.

China is buying the land of other countries now. I think this is the first step of intruding on other countries. However, the next "emperor" or president, Xi Jinping, does not have enough knowledge in economics so he won't know what will come next. That is why China's tendency is usually to return to the problem of Japan's history. It will continue to say, "Japan was bad. Japan has the 'original sin.' That's the source of all the evil in the world."

Therefore, we must bear these bad, ill words from them this year and the next. We need some kind of tolerance and perseverance, continuous effort to keep our pride, to keep our economic strength, and to keep our will to protect our country.

China will dissolve starting from Hong Kong
I think the scene we will see in the near future will be quite different.

I already said about a lot of bad phenomena that will surround Japan in the near future. *Naoki Komuro's Great Prediction* (IRH Press Co., Ltd., 2012), on the other hand, already says that China will make a great mistake in the near future and will dissolve its huge country and fall apart.

One of the starting points is Hong Kong. China, of course, wants to absorb Hong Kong and Taiwan, and wants to put them in the same condition as mainland China. But the top leader of Hong Kong refused the educational policy from mainland China, saying that it doesn't have enough good quality content and that the people of Hong Kong will suffer a lot from the textbook policy of Beijing, China.

So the new way has already begun in Hong Kong and Taiwan will follow this movement.

4 South Korea Needs to Consider Itself as "A Member of the West"

The famous Senkaku Islands will be the symbol of diplomatic struggle.

The attitude of the Japanese government is not usual. Prime Minister Noda is like a very heavy sumo wrestler; he's being pushed and pushed but just isn't moving. China is astonished by that.

South Korea did almost the same thing this August,☆ yet they said, "The Chinese are rude people and are barbarians. We are not so. We

---

☆ Former President Lee Myung-bak landed on Takeshima and he also demanded an apology from the Emperor of Japan.

Power to the Future

are gentlemen-like." They said this and laughed at the Chinese people.

It's incredible. I can't understand but maybe there is a little difference. I hope there is.

South Korean people are persuaded by the United States and also by Japan. We are colleagues on military bases, economic bases and in terms of political systems. In this sense, we are quite different from North Korea and China. This is a very large and tall barrier, enough to cause collisions between several countries.

We belong to a Western political and economic policy and system, which have been prevailing.

5 We Must Gain the Strength to Conquer Evil

China does not understand the meaning of liberty

Now it seems that, in these twenty years, a different form of communism was developed in China and conquered Japan. Also it is aiming toward conquering the United States of America. However, in the next few years, China's economic debacle will deepen further and further like the Mariana Trench. It will go down to the deep sea, and at that time China should be taught that the world economy consists of cooperation and co-assisting between each country, and that the main policy of Western society is based on liberty.

China still does not understand the meaning of liberty. That is why our magazine, *The Liberty*, should be read in mainland China (laughs) so the people can understand the meaning of liberty.

The meaning of liberty comes from the Will of God.

The Will of God was to make human beings as His children. Being "God's child" means that each human being equally has a right to be good, a right to prosper, and a right to become the light of Heaven through making effort. That is the meaning of liberty.

In mainland China, Chinese people can never understand this meaning. They are seeking for the economic meaning of liberty after the change in economic policy of the nation. China's political policy is still Marxism-Leninism. China should know now that its political system and economic freedom cannot be compatible.

Fight against bad systems which are not loved by God

What I want to realize now is this: if we, the Japanese, could fight only in terms of values, philosophy, political and economic systems, and in the meaning of a new history, we are to fight against bad systems which are not loved by God. I believe so.

I dare say that the Japanese government, of course the Japanese mass media and the Japanese people, must combine their powers together to conquer evil intrusion or bad conceptions from the North. We must protect ourselves from the evil power that wants to spread all over the world. Also, we must protect good things, good traditions, good people and good economic systems from the evil power that wants to kill these things.

We must fight against this current. We, the Japanese, can do that.

The Happiness Realization Party and Happy Science have been fighting the past few years and we will continue to fight against the enemy of God.

We must be strong. We must get stronger and stronger until we can conquer evil. That is the conclusion of this lecture.

Power to the Future

(和訳) 第3章　未来に力を

1　世界の未来に関する「三つの仮説」

　よくよく、あなたがたに言っておきます。

　今日の説法である「未来に力を」は、大きなテーマであり、私たちの未来の行き先を決定するでしょう。その未来とは、日本を含めた、世界のすべての国々の未来です。

　私たち日本人は今、逆境のなかにあります。今が転換期なのです。

　ある人たちは、「台頭する中国が、日本をのみ込み、侵略するだろう。また、国際社会には、政治力や軍事力などが働いているが、中国は、そうしたすべての力に打ち勝って、次の『世界の支配者』になるだろう」と言っています。これが一つの仮

説です。

　また、別の仮説では、「アメリカ合衆国が力を盛り返し、同盟国と協力して、台頭する新しい侵略勢力、つまり中国や北朝鮮などの帝国主義から自分たちを守る」というものがあります。これが、もう一つのシナリオです。

　そして、三つ目の仮説は、日本自体にかかわるものです。すなわち、「私たち日本は、自ら決断し、自らの足で立ち上がって、アジア・オセアニア地域を守り、世界の危機を平和と繁栄に変えていくべきである」というものです。これが三つ目の戦略です。

　これについて述べていきましょう。

Power to the Future

2 経済において縮小政策をとる欧米

日本には、まだまだ「未来の可能性」がある

私は、今回の演題に「未来に力を」と付けました。これは、「私たちには、未来を変えるための『力』が必要である。その『力』自体、未来を変えることを要請するのだ」ということと、「未来においては、当然、今以上の『力』が必要になってくる」ということを意味しています。

ここで言う「力」とは、数多くの意味を含んでいます。

例えば、今、日本で、IMF（国際通貨基金）の会合が開かれており、世界から２万人以上の人々が集まっています（説法当時）。

当初は、エジプトで開催される予定でしたが、

Power to the Future

大規模デモの余波で大混乱の最中にあるため、日本は、エジプトの代わりに引き受け、世界中から数多くの人を招いたのです。

そして、日本は、世界の人々に、「これが未来のスタイルであり、新しい未来の姿なのだ」ということを見せていました。

他のアジア諸国や中南米、アフリカ、ヨーロッパから来た人々は、「ああ、日本には潜在的な力がある。日本には、まだまだ『未来の可能性』がある」と言っていました。

「1990年代の日本」に学ぶべき欧州連合

初日、私の印象に強く残ったのは、IMF総会の参加メンバーで、ヨーロッパから来たある重要人物が、「私たちは、『不良債権問題に対する1990年代の日本の対応（金融機関への公的資金の投入）

Power to the Future

はあまりよくなかった』と主張していたが、今では、『日本はよくやった』と思っている。私たちヨーロッパの人々も、日本から学び、日本の政策に追いつかなければならない」というようにコメントしていたことです。

世界は今、経済衰退の危機に瀕しています。

例えば、昨日、ＩＭＦは、「ユーロ圏の銀行は、約350兆円の融資を世界中から引き上げるだろう」と述べていました。これは非常に巨大な額です。

しかし、「融資額を削減する」ということは、「アフリカやアジアの一部、さらに、その他の地域の途上国への融資を削減する」ということです。つまり、欧州連合は、彼らの義務を十分に果たすことができなくなるのです。

そのため、ある人は、「日本は円高政策をとっており、今は円高なので（説法当時）、日本であれば、

Power to the Future

他の国々を支援できる」と述べていました。たいへん重い責任ですが、非常に大事なことだと思います。

もし、ユーロ圏の銀行が融資を引き上げて、単に自分たちのバランスシート（貸借対照表）を健全化することだけに集中したならば、彼らの銀行は、データ上、よくなるでしょうが、世界経済は、ナイアガラの滝のように落ちていくでしょう。

十分な経済政策を持っていないオバマ氏

次の問題は、もちろん、「アメリカ経済」です。

大統領選の時期が迫っており、ロムニー氏とオバマ氏の接戦となっていますが（説法当時）、二人とも十分な政策がないと思います。

オバマ氏は、アメリカの財政赤字を最小限にしたいと考えているでしょう。

Power to the Future

　一方、ミット・ロムニー氏は、大きな政府を小さな政府に変えようとするでしょう。それは、彼の緊急経済政策には予算削減が伴うことを意味します。

　ロムニー氏は、オバマ氏よりも軍事費を使うだろうと思いますが、確実に、「小さな政府」政策を目指していくでしょう。それが、共和党の伝統的な考え方だからです。

　このように、欧州連合とアメリカ合衆国の両者とも、経済においては縮小政策を目指しているのです。

3　経済崩壊の危機に瀕する中国

中国には、金融についての
「知識と経験」が足りない

　さらなる問題は、「中国」でしょう。

　これは、単なる私の推測にすぎませんが、中国は、おそらく、金融についての知識と経験を十分に持っていないと思います。というのも、彼らは、ここ20年間の巨大な高度経済成長を経験しただけだからです。

　それ以前、彼らは、非常に原始的な経済、すなわち農業国レベルの経済しか持っていませんでした。

　つまり、彼らは今、初めて、経済の"崖"から転落する危機に直面し、経済崩壊の瀬戸際に立って

Power to the Future

いるのです。

　これは、彼らにとって初めての経験です。彼らは、数多くの苦しみを余儀なくさせられるでしょう。数多くの逆境を味わうと思います。なぜなら、このような経済衰退の例は、彼らの歴史上、少なくとも、ここ100年間にはなかったことだからです。

　彼らは今、日本から学ぶべきです。日本は、「いかに金融の方向をコントロールするか」ということについて中国を指導できるのです。

　しかし、彼らは、聞く耳を持たないでしょうから、国の経済政策の舵取りを誤ると思います。

日本が「中国の侵略」を防ぐために必要なこと

　この中国の経済崩壊の危機は、2011年から始まっており、2012年の今、徐々に大きくなってきて

います。ただ、彼らは、それについて、あまり考えてはいません。「それは景気循環の一部である。今は下降に向かっているかもしれないが、来年あるいは2～3年以内に再びよくなってくるはずだ」と信じているのです。

そして、これまで以上の多額の資金を軍事力に投入し、その軍事費を、他国を占領したり、脅迫したりして、原油や鉄・その他の金属等の資源を得ることに変えようとしています。

さらに、彼らは今、他国での土地購入も進めています。これは、他の国々への侵略の第一歩であると思われます。

しかし、次の"皇帝"、いや、次の国家主席である習近平は、十分な経済知識を持っていないので、次に何が起こるかが分からないでしょう。

そのため、彼らは、いつも日本の歴史問題に帰

っていくのです。「日本が悪かったのだ。日本には原罪があるのだ。そこに世界の諸悪の根源がある」。そう彼らは言い続けることでしょう。

したがって、今年（2012年）と来年（2013年）は、このような悪口に、私たちは耐えなければなりません。

私たちには、ある種の寛容と忍耐、そして、「誇りを保つ」「強い経済を維持する」「『自らの国を守る』という意志を持ち続ける」という、たゆまぬ努力が必要です。

中国の解体は「香港」から始まる

私が思うに、私たちが近未来に見る光景は、まったく違ったものとなるでしょう。

私は、すでに、近未来において日本を取り巻くであろう数多くの悪い現象について言及しました

Power to the Future

が、一方で、『小室直樹の大予言』(大川隆法著、幸福の科学出版刊)には、「中国は、近い将来、大きな間違いを犯し、その巨大な国は自ら解体していく」と述べられています。

その始まりの一つは、「香港」です。

中国は、当然、「香港と台湾を吸収し、中国本土と同じようにしたい」と思っていますが、香港では、最近、そのトップが、中国本土の教育政策の導入を拒否しました。

彼は、「北京政府の教科書政策は、内容が十分ではない。これでは、香港の人々は多くの悪影響を受けるだろう」と語ったのです。

このように、香港から、すでに新しい道が開けています。台湾もこの動きに続くでしょう。

Power to the Future

4　韓国は「西側の一員」としての自覚を

　また、有名な尖閣諸島は、争いの象徴となるでしょう。

　日本政府の態度はいつもと違います。野田首相（説法当時）は、体重の重い相撲取りのようで、押されても押されても微動だにしません。中国は、その態度に驚いています。

　一方、韓国の人たちは、この８月に、中国と同じようなこと（李明博・前大統領による竹島上陸や天皇謝罪要求発言）をしたにもかかわらず、「中国人は失礼な人々だ。彼らは野蛮だが、私たちは違う。私たちは紳士的である」と言って、中国人のことを笑っていました。

　信じられません。よく分かりませんが、多少の

違いがあるのでしょう。そう願いたいものです。

　韓国は、アメリカや日本に説得されています。私たちは、軍事面においても、経済面においても、さらには政治体制においても、仲間であり、北朝鮮や中国とはまったく違うのです。これは、非常に大きくて高い障壁であり、それによって、幾つかの国との間で衝突が起きているほどです。

　私たちは西側の政治経済体制に属しています。そして、それが、優勢であり続けているのです。

5　悪を打ち負かす「強さ」を身につけよ

「自由」の意味が分かっていない中国

　現在、「ここ20年ほどで、中国の、異なるタイプの共産主義が日本を席巻し、アメリカ合衆国の征服も目指している」というように見えますが、

Power to the Future

　ここ数年の間にも、中国経済の崩壊は拡大し、マリアナ海溝のような"深い海"に沈んでいくでしょう。

　そのとき、彼らは、「世界経済は各国の協力と支えによって成り立っており、西側社会の主要な方針は自由に基づいているのだ」ということを学ぶでしょう。

　彼らは、まだ自由の意味が分かっていません。私たちの雑誌「ザ・リバティ」（幸福の科学出版刊）は、中国本土でも読まれるべきですね（笑）。そうすれば、自由の意味が分かるでしょう。

　自由の意味は、神の意志に由来します。

　神の意志とは、「神は、人間を神の子として創った」という意味です。そして、神の子とは、「一人ひとりが、善なる存在となる権利、繁栄する権利、努力して天上界の光となれる権利を等しく持っている」ということを意味します。これが自由の意

Power to the Future

味なのです。

　中国本土の人々は、この意味が分かっていません。彼らは、国の経済政策が変わって以降、経済面における自由しか求めていないのです。

　彼らの政治体制は、いまだにマルクス・レーニン主義です。「これは、経済的自由とは両立しえないのだ」ということを、彼らは知らなければなりません。

神に愛されていない「悪(あ)しき体制」と戦え

　私が今、実現したいのは、こういうことです。

　もし、私たち日本人が、価値観や思想、政治体制、経済体制、新しい歴史観においてのみ戦うことができるのであるならば、私たちは、神に愛されていない「悪(あ)しき体制」と戦うべきです。そう思います。

Power to the Future

　ですから、私は、あえて申し上げます。

　日本政府、そして、もちろん日本のマスコミと日本の国民は、力を合わせて、「北」からの悪しき侵略(しんりゃく)や悪しき思想を打ち破り、「世界に広がろうとする悪の勢力」「数多くの、よきもの、よき伝統、よき人々、よき経済体制を破壊しようとする悪の勢力」から身を守らなければなりません。

　私たちは、こうした趨勢(すうせい)に対して戦わなければならないのです。私たち日本人には、それができます。

　幸福実現党と幸福の科学は、ここ数年、戦い続けていますが、これからも、「神の敵」と戦っていくつもりです。

　私たちは、強くあらねばなりません。もっともっと強くなって、悪を打ち負かさなければならないのです。

Power to the Future

これが本日の結論です。

References by Ryuho Okawa

- *The Great Unification of Politics and Religion*
    (IRH Press Co., Ltd., 2012)

- *Naoki Komuro's Great Prediction*
    (IRH Press Co., Ltd., 2012)

- *Zhou Enlai's Prediction*
    (IRH Press Co., Ltd., 2012)

- *The Power of Religion that Protects Nation*
    (The Happiness Realization Party, 2012)

China's Hidden Agenda: The Mastermind Behind the Anti-American and Anti-Japanese Protests
    (IRH Press Co., Ltd., 2012)

- Available only in Japanese

『Power to the Future』
大川隆法著作参考文献

『政治と宗教の大統合』(幸福の科学出版刊)

『小室直樹の大予言』(同上)

『周恩来の予言』(同上)

『国を守る宗教の力』(幸福実現党刊)

『中国と習近平に未来はあるか』(同上)

Power to the Future ──未来に力を──
<ruby>パワー トゥ ザ フューチャー</ruby>

2013年3月29日　初版第1刷

著　者　　大川隆法
発行所　　幸福の科学出版株式会社

〒107-0052　東京都港区赤坂2丁目10番14号
TEL(03)5573-7700
http://www.irhpress.co.jp/

印刷・製本　　株式会社 堀内印刷所

落丁・乱丁本はおとりかえいたします
©Ryuho Okawa 2013. Printed in Japan. 検印省略
ISBN978-4-86395-318-5 C0014

大川隆法ベストセラーズ・豊かな人生のために

英語が開く「人生論」「仕事論」
知的幸福実現論

あなたの英語力が、この国の未来を救う――。国際的な視野と交渉力を身につけ、あなたの英語力を飛躍的にアップさせる秘訣が満載。

1,400円

サバイバルする社員の条件
リストラされない幸福の防波堤

能力だけでは生き残れない。不況の時代にリストラされないためのサバイバル術が語られる。この一冊が、リストラからあなたを守る！

1,400円

生涯現役人生
100歳まで幸福に生きる心得

「毎日楽しい」「死ぬまで元気」、そんな老後を送るには――。長寿を得て幸福に生きる心得を、仏陀がやさしい言葉で語られる。

1,500円

幸福の科学出版

大川隆法 ベストセラーズ・世界伝道の軌跡

大川隆法
オーストラリア 巡錫の軌跡

親中路線に傾くオーストラリア──。2009年3月と2012年10月の2度にわたる巡錫と英語説法がオーストラリアの国論を変えた。その歴史的瞬間と感動を振り返る。

1,300円

大川隆法
ウガンダ 巡錫の軌跡

2012年6月、不惜身命で貫いた海外巡錫が、ついに5大陸制覇の偉業となった。アフリカの地ウガンダに、「希望の光」を灯した、記念すべき巡錫の記録。

1,300円

大川隆法
スリランカ 巡錫の軌跡

2011年11月、仏教の本場スリランカで、再誕の仏陀が新たな法を説かれた。アジア・ミッションを締めくくる、同年7カ国目での巡錫の記録。

1,300円

※表示価格は本体価格(税別)です。

大川隆法 ベストセラーズ・世界の指導者の本心

バラク・オバマの スピリチュアル・メッセージ
再選大統領は世界に平和をもたらすか

弱者救済と軍事費削減、富裕層への増税……。再選翌日のオバマ大統領守護霊インタビューを緊急刊行！日本の国防危機が明らかになる。
【幸福実現党刊】

1,400円

ロシア・プーチン 新大統領と帝国の未来
守護霊インタヴュー

中国が覇権主義を拡大させるなか、ロシアはどんな国家戦略をとるのか!? また、親日家プーチン氏の意外な過去世も明らかに。
【幸福実現党刊】

1,300円

安倍新総理 スピリチュアル・インタビュー
復活総理の勇気と覚悟を問う

自民党政権に、日本を守り抜く覚悟はあるか!? 衆院選翌日、マスコミや国民がもっとも知りたい新総理の本心を問う、安倍氏守護霊インタビュー。
【幸福実現党刊】

1,400円

幸福の科学出版

大川隆法ベストセラーズ・中国の野望を見抜く

小室直樹の大予言
2015年 中華帝国の崩壊

世界征服か？ 内部崩壊か？ 孤高の国際政治学者・小室直樹が、習近平氏の国家戦略と中国の矛盾を分析。日本に国防の秘策を授ける。

1,400円

周恩来の予言
新中華帝国の隠れたる神

北朝鮮のミサイル問題の背後には、中国の思惑があった！ 現代中国を霊界から指導する周恩来が語った、戦慄の世界覇権戦略とは!?

1,400円

中国と習近平に未来はあるか
反日デモの謎を解く

「反日デモ」も、「反原発・沖縄基地問題」も中国が仕組んだ日本占領への布石だった。緊迫する日中関係の未来を習近平氏守護霊に問う。
【幸福実現党刊】

1,400円

※表示価格は本体価格（税別）です。

大川隆法ベストセラーズ・希望の未来を切り拓く

未来の法
新たなる地球世紀へ

序　章　勝利への道
　　　　——「思いの力」に目覚めよ

第1章　成功学入門
　　　　——理想を実現するための考え方

第2章　心が折れてたまるか
　　　　——「強い心」を発見すれば未来が変わる

第3章　積極的に生きる
　　　　——失敗を恐れず、チャレンジし続けよう

第4章　未来を創る力
　　　　——新しい時代を切り拓くために

第5章　希望の復活
　　　　——さらなる未来の発展を目指して

2,000円

法シリーズ19作目

暗い世相に負けるな！　悲観的な自己像に縛られるな！　心に眠る「無限のパワー」に目覚めよ！　人類の未来を拓く鍵は、私たち一人ひとりの心のなかにある。

教育の使命
世界をリードする人材の輩出を

わかりやすい切り口で、幸福の科学の教育思想が語られた一書。イジメ問題や、教育荒廃に対する最終的な答えが、ここにある。

1,800円

幸福の科学出版

大川隆法 ベストセラーズ・国難を打破する

されど光はここにある
天災と人災を超えて

被災地・東北で説かれた説法を収録。東日本大震災が日本に遺した教訓とは。悲劇を乗り越え、希望の未来を創りだす方法が綴られる。

1,600円

政治と宗教の大統合
今こそ、「新しい国づくり」を

国家の危機が迫るなか、全国民に向けて、日本人の精神構造を変える「根本的な国づくり」の必要性を訴える書。

1,800円

国を守る宗教の力
この国に正論と正義を

3年前から国防と経済の危機を警告してきた国師が、迷走する日本を一喝! 国難を打破し、日本を復活させる正論を訴える。
【幸福実現党刊】

1,500円

※表示価格は本体価格(税別)です。

幸福の科学グループのご案内

宗教、教育、政治、出版などの活動を通じて、地球的ユートピアの実現を目指しています。

宗教法人　幸福の科学

1986年に立宗。1991年に宗教法人格を取得。信仰の対象は、地球系霊団の最高大霊、主エル・カンターレ。世界100カ国以上の国々に信者を持ち、全人類救済という尊い使命のもと、信者は、「愛」と「悟り」と「ユートピア建設」の教えの実践、伝道に励んでいます。

（2013年3月現在）

愛

幸福の科学の「愛」とは、与える愛です。これは、仏教の慈悲や布施の精神と同じことです。信者は、仏法真理をお伝えすることを通して、多くの方に幸福な人生を送っていただくための活動に励んでいます。

悟り

「悟り」とは、自らが仏の子であることを知るということです。教学や精神統一によって心を磨き、智慧を得て悩みを解決すると共に、天使・菩薩の境地を目指し、より多くの人を救える力を身につけていきます。

ユートピア建設

私たち人間は、地上に理想世界を建設するという尊い使命を持って生まれてきています。社会の悪を押しとどめ、善を推し進めるために、信者はさまざまな活動に積極的に参加しています。

海外支援・災害支援

国内外の世界で貧困や災害、心の病で苦しんでいる人々に対しては、現地メンバーや支援団体と連携して、物心両面にわたり、あらゆる手段で手を差し伸べています。

自殺を減らそうキャンペーン

年間約3万人の自殺者を減らすため、全国各地で街頭キャンペーンを展開しています。

公式サイト **www.withyou-hs.net**

ヘレンの会

ヘレン・ケラーを理想として活動する、ハンディキャップを持つ方とボランティアの会です。視聴覚障害者、肢体不自由な方々に仏法真理を学んでいただくための、さまざまなサポートをしています。

公式サイト **www.helen-hs.net**

INFORMATION

お近くの精舎・支部・拠点など、お問い合わせは、こちらまで！
幸福の科学サービスセンター
TEL. **03-5793-1727** (受付時間 火〜金：10〜20時／土・日：10〜18時)
宗教法人 幸福の科学公式サイト **happy-science.jp**

教育

学校法人 幸福の科学学園

学校法人 幸福の科学学園は、幸福の科学の教育理念のもとにつくられた教育機関です。人間にとって最も大切な宗教教育の導入を通じて精神性を高めながら、ユートピア建設に貢献する人材輩出を目指しています。

幸福の科学学園

中学校・高等学校（那須本校）
2010年4月開校・栃木県那須郡（男女共学・全寮制）
TEL **0287-75-7777**
公式サイト **happy-science.ac.jp**

関西中学校・高等学校（関西校）
2013年4月開校・滋賀県大津市（男女共学・寮及び通学）
TEL **077-573-7774**
公式サイト **kansai.happy-science.ac.jp**

幸福の科学大学（仮称・設置認可申請予定）
2015年開学予定
TEL **03-6277-7248**（幸福の科学 大学準備室）
公式サイト **university.happy-science.jp**

仏法真理塾「サクセスNo.1」
小・中・高校生が、信仰教育を基礎にしながら、「勉強も『心の修行』」と考えて学んでいます。
TEL **03-5750-0747**（東京本校）

不登校児支援スクール「ネバー・マインド」
心の面からのアプローチを重視して、不登校の子供たちを支援しています。
また、障害児支援の「**ユー・アー・エンゼル！**」運動も行っています。
TEL **03-5750-1741**

エンゼルプランV
幼少時からの心の教育を大切にして、信仰をベースにした幼児教育を行っています。
TEL **03-5750-0757**

NPO活動支援

学校からのいじめ追放を目指し、さまざまな社会提言をしています。また、各地でのシンポジウムや学校への啓発ポスター掲示等に取り組むNPO「いじめから子供を守ろう！ネットワーク」を支援しています。

公式サイト **mamoro.org**
ブログ **mamoro.blog86.fc2.com**
相談窓口 TEL **03-5719-2170**

政治

幸福実現党

内憂外患(ないゆうがいかん)の国難に立ち向かうべく、2009年5月に幸福実現党を立党しました。創立者である大川隆法党総裁の精神的指導のもと、宗教だけでは解決できない問題に取り組み、幸福を具体化するための力になっています。

党員の機関紙
「幸福実現NEWS」

TEL 03-6441-0754
公式サイト hr-party.jp

出版メディア事業

幸福の科学出版

大川隆法総裁の仏法真理の書を中心に、ビジネス、自己啓発、小説など、さまざまなジャンルの書籍・雑誌を出版しています。他にも、映画事業、文学・学術発展のための振興事業、テレビ・ラジオ番組の提供など、幸福の科学文化を広げる事業を行っています。

TEL 03-5573-7700
公式サイト irhpress.co.jp

入 会 の ご 案 内

あなたも、幸福の科学に集い、ほんとうの幸福を見つけてみませんか？

幸福の科学では、大川隆法総裁が説く仏法真理をもとに、
「どうすれば幸福になれるのか、また、
他の人を幸福にできるのか」を学び、実践しています。

入会

大川隆法総裁の教えを信じ、学ぼうとする方なら、どなたでも入会できます。入会された方には、『入会版「正心法語」』が授与されます。（入会の奉納は1,000円目安です）

ネットでも入会できます。詳しくは、下記URLへ。
happy-science.jp/joinus

三帰誓願

仏弟子としてさらに信仰を深めたい方は、仏・法・僧の三宝への帰依を誓う「三帰誓願式」を受けることができます。三帰誓願者には、『仏説・正心法語』『祈願文①』『祈願文②』『エル・カンターレへの祈り』が授与されます。

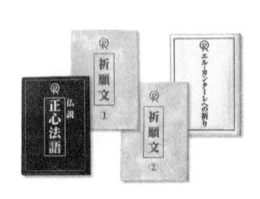

植福の会

植福は、ユートピア建設のために、自分の富を差し出す尊い布施の行為です。布施の機会として、毎月1口1,000円からお申込みいただける、「植福の会」がございます。

「植福の会」に参加された方のうちご希望の方には、幸福の科学の小冊子（毎月1回）をお送りいたします。詳しくは、下記の電話番号までお問い合わせください。

月刊「幸福の科学」
ザ・伝道 
ヤング・ブッダ 
ヘルメス・エンゼルズ 

INFORMATION

幸福の科学サービスセンター
TEL. 03-5793-1727（受付時間 火〜金：10〜20時／土・日：10〜18時）
宗教法人 幸福の科学 公式サイト **happy-science.jp**